An inspirational book to help
with the journey of care

BY CARA BARILLA

"Eternal Nurture - An inspirational book to help with the journey of Care"

By Cara Barilla

ISBN: 9780645285154

Copyright Cara Barilla 2023

All rights reserved 2023

Little Lemon Book Co. Syd

www.littlelemonbookco.com.au

SYDNEY

Graphic art illustrations by Cara Barilla

Graphic art editing by Jessica Chaplin

jesschaplincreative.com.au

AuthorCaraBarilla.com.au

This book is available in quantity for your group or organisation

For more information, please contact Little Lemon Book Co.

Printed in Australia.

No part of this publication may be reproduced in whole or in part or stored in a retrieval system or transmitted in any form or by any means, electronic, mechanical, photocopying, recording or otherwise without written permission of the publisher.

Genre; Gift book. Adult / Mature reading / Spiritual / New age. First Edition 2023

For my Grandmère; Thank you for showing me the purest forms of Nurture

"The pure simplicity of a smile can connect and trigger beautiful forces"

"Closing your eyes and embracing in a true hug can transport you into another universe"

"Allow your eyes to smile"

"To nurture is to give love through service."

"The sincerity of nurture can set spirits free."

"Allow your spirit to embrace
the beauty of care."

"When you care for someone unconditionally, they are receiving a pure heavenly source."

"When we give a piece of kindness to one,
it will be passed on for years to come."

"A simple smile can heal inner wounds."

"A nurturing soul is like a lighthouse for heaven to see."

"It's impossible to help everyone but possible to nurture few."

"There is nothing more wholesome than to embrace the arms of assistance."

"Close your eyes and feel kindness."

"A nurturing soul can live in planes which reach many worlds."

"When you offer help to someone, thoughts of gratitude will multiply."

"It costs nothing to be kind, smile at another and live in pure grace."

"You can be the shining star
in someone's dark night."

"When you lend a helping hand,
you'll receive back a helping heart."

"Nurture your soul with love, respect and passion."

"When you nurture your mind with your heart, you'll see a new source of nurture come into your life."

"You're never too old to nurture your heart with dancing, singing and laughter."

"Nurture your inner child by play; you can still live playfully and experience joy."

"Deep thoughts of happy memories
can nurture spirit."

"Nurture a friend by a call, message or a spontaneous gift."

"How would you use your five senses
to experience self-nurture?"

"Listening to the healing sounds of nature can nurture away unnecessary thoughts."

"An unconditional hug is a lifelong gift."

"Nurture your future self by making loving and joyful memories today."

"When you nurture others through the bliss of a laugh, hug, smile or unconditional service you are healing a piece of your inner child."

"A life with self-nurture comes a satisfied inner child."

"It takes a wholesome soul to love with unconditional nurture."

"A soul that offers pure service
is one of God's people."

"The sincerity of a smile is a hug in itself."

"Unconditional love isn't perfect and the relationship which you'll grow to become is self-nurturing."

"When giving service to others you are taking away a piece of yourself. Your time, energy and unique methods of service is eternally given away into treasured memories."

"When there is unconditional nurture there is an unbreakable bond between two people."

"The essence of someone's assistance can be expressed through eye contact, a touch, kind words and a nurturing task."

"No act of nurture to another will ever be wasted; regardless of how big or small. There's a little piece of them which was healed in that very instant."

"The power of nurture can save lives,
embrace pure love and heal away darkness."

"The simplicity of helping a friend will never be forgotten."

"Nurturing starts with accepting nurture back into your heart."

"The greatest act of all is an applaud,
a smile, a congratulations and a support"

"Sometimes it's ok to say no to today. Take your time back, nurture yourself and prepare for a new tomorrow."

"Self-love comes with saying yes to self-respect."

"Nurture mostly comes when not expecting nurture in return."

"To nurture one's soul is as simple as giving yourself patience."

"We are merely here to help others
and save each other."

"A little piece of your good deed will save a stranger. For good deeds will continue to travel as long as time exists."

"Lifting up the light in others
is another seen sunrise."

"Our essence is truly alight when we nurture the lives of others. Whether it be through service, words, giving or a simply welcoming smile."

"Nurture is the soul reaching the surface"

"The nurture we receive determines the way we grow."

"Nurture your mind and your soul will blossom."

"The way we nurture our relationships is a pillar to the way we give love."

"Nurturing your dreams everyday will wholeheartedly add fuel for your success."

"To nurture one's creativity, is a gateway to new worlds of imagination."

"When we nurture our health,
we strengthen our pillar to well-being."

"Nurture your inner passions for they are the true essence of your life purpose."

"When we give care to ourselves and our need to absorb through curiosity, is the foundation for learning."

"When we offer nurture to our self-esteem, the core of your confidence will alight"

"Nurturing the ability to be kind again to others and yourself, will feed your heart with compassion."

"When we live our life through embracing our sense of humour; our inner-child will forever be nurtured with joy"

"To nurture your inner child; is the essence to living with the purest joy in life."

"When we nurture our spirit with gratitude, we are giving pure guidance in our journey of life."

"Caring for ourselves by giving time to our unique talents, are great sources to self-nurture."

"Your inner feeling of gratitude will be comforted once used in vocal and visual practice"

"Healthy communication lies within nurturing your inner truth"

"Change can take place when you comfort your methods of flexibility."

"Hurdling over the many challenges of life can be nourished with resilience."

"Self-care and self-nurture can be nurtured when you give others boundaries to your needs."

"You can nurture your spirit always with eternal hope. This will alight pure faith."

"When we are mindful of our surroundings, we can understand new ways to nurture ourselves within any social settings; through any form of your nurturing senses."

"We can always nurture our goals to unlock new passions in life; We just need to focus and trust our pathway of instinct."

"The movement of growth in life cycles can be nurtured through courage and motivation."

"Nurture your imagination each day through the creative magic of visualization."

"Our sense of inner peace can be nurtured at any place and anytime through the power of self-love; allow this feeling to give yourself permission to let go and exude confidence to the world."

"When we travel the world, we nurture a part of our spirit which wants to connect to the truth and culture of life."

"The unconditional care for others isn't just through actions or words; but can be felt through pure presence and eye contact."

"When we give our time to others to care for them, we are giving others the endless possibility to alight humanity."

"The amounts of times that we nurture ourselves is shined through the people who have once nurtured us."

"The priceless gift of a hug can heal trauma
and bring hope inside one's heart."

"When we bring joy to others we are enriching ourselves with the beauty of the sun's power; to shine and to spread warmth of light."

"Hope is spread through smiles."

"The energy you offer to someone is sacred. Release your energy to the people who would release their energy to you unconditionally."

"We can shift the world; one smile at a time."

"A simple act of kindness can shift many lives and heal many traumas."

"Helping others is the key to unlocking true happiness and fulfillment."

"We offer love to others not to only receive it back; to give back to humanity."

"The assistance we offer to people is a lifetime gift of time and nurture"

"We rise by lifting up others through our five senses."

"A rich life is a well-nurtured one"

"The power of serving others is a humane rite of passage."

"The key to finding our core selves is to lose ourselves in the nurture of others."

"Giving back to others with the power of gratitude can help amplify their need to serve."

"As long as we are by their side,
they will feel loved."

"In life we make a living,
but in service we make a purpose."

"Kindness is a universal language;
you don't have to see it to feel it,
nor do you have to hear it to see it."

"The world needs more acts of service and less judgement."

"Patience and presence together
is a beautifully bound gift."

"If we have ever helped to find someone's life purpose; then we've nurtured ours."

"Our purpose in life is to help others find theirs."

"A kind word or gesture can lift up someone's vibration in ways we can't measure."

"The core value of our life experience is not in what we accumulate, but in what we contribute."

"Our life's legacy is not in what we actually leave behind; though how many lives we have touched."

"The gift of being able to help others
is a testament to our humanity."

"The best way to show gratitude is to nurture others back."

"One small kind gesture here can ripple to thousands of smiles there."

"Kindness has no measure.
You simply give kindness great or small."

"Nurturing others is a foundation of a hearty and compassionate community."

"The world needs more humanitarians and less celebrities."

"Nurture and empathy are open doors to strengthen the best version of ourselves as human beings."

"Making a positive difference charges the world with hope."

"I am worthy of self-love;
I am ready to heal and nurture myself."

"In a world where you can be anything,
be compassionate and helpful."

"When we give to others, we create a ripple effect of positive change."

"The only way forward is to care for those who need pure love and nurture."

"The greatest investment for a humble and wise life is to empathise, use compassion and patience."

"The loving energy we naturally offer to others is always unforeseen; for it is hidden through millions of unique facial expressions, words, eye contact, acts of service and body language."

"Take time to slowdown for your self-nurture. Sometimes it is when you anchor down in pure presence that you can truly accept and give pure nurture."

"We are all one and can reflect our own flaws off each other. When you see this, it is your opportunity to balance with care, understanding and acceptance."

"When we smile, we charge new opportunities to open energies."

"The way to self-care is when we offer care without the expectation of a two-way street."

"Loving eye contact can heal hundreds of nerves at once."

"When we accept nature in all of its pure essence, we can accept ourselves within all of our differences."

"The purest act of accepting someone unconditionally can heal and nurture inner worlds."

"We all have gifts to give; time, care, eye contact, acts of service, hugs and a listening and compassionate ear."

"Don't forget to walk away from those who don't unconditionally support you. It's okay to cut off toxic connections."

"Sacred solitude can assist you with healing away traumas and guiding yourself to the right path."

"Your surroundings are a reflection of your current lifestyle and thoughts. If you want a new tomorrow, paint a new today."

"Music has a way to hug the soul and rejoice with someone within musical nurture."

"Your heart is a sacred tool to connect, heal, translate, guide and recharge."

"When we meet people from all over the world we can connect, rejoice, teach and accept each other for our unique pathway."

"It is a true gift to be able to care for one's heart."

"To bring joy to another life is a wonderful way to evolve through kindness."

"We are all able to heal others through voice, words, physical touch, service and presence. When we practice this act in our life we are able to grow in soul and life experience."

"Have you made someone laugh
or smile today?"

"Don't forget to thank those who have given you light and nurture into your life."

"We are all one and can all share the purest joys of a compassionate life."

"Emotional nurture goes hand in hand with physical nurture."

"We can change the way we view life by changing the way we give and receive our life to others."

"The ultimate act of nurture is sacrificing a piece of your soul for another's happiness."

"We can change the world one hug at a time."

"Your inner harnessed love is always there and is there for unlimited service."

"Sometimes nurturing others feels like a sore back, rough hands and sore feet."

"For unconditional love, we keep going."

"Always thank those who sacrificed their own needs to help yours."

"Love that we give sometimes isn't seen or heard."

"When we use our heart to help others, we can truly find our language of nurture."

"Offering the sincerest love to others can be through the smallest of gestures."

"Our most cherished memories of nurture can often be shown through our current language of nurture to others."

"Sometimes it's a special gift to yourself when you offer someone else a piece of your heart."

"Your presence and sincerity may be
a beautiful gift to someone else."

"Being there for someone is a sacred exchange of energy. A truly special gift."

"To give back to the community is giving back
a piece of old wisdom to your soul."

"We can care for humanity one at a time.
For the quality of our support can spread
far and fast."

"You can cradle anyone; For words can cradle a heart; A hug can cradle a soul and hearty food can nurture their temple."

"To practice empathy is a key ingredient for a nurtured soul."

"A kind heart can travel further and faster than any form of transportation."

"Being there for others is a way to show them that they have a little part of you in them. A piece of your heart."

"You are a reflection of your surroundings and can choose how you want to be nurtured. How do you treat your surroundings?"

"True humanitarianism is gifted
deep within the act of service."

"The act of patience can heal and support others."

"A gracious soul is one of the most beautiful acts of living."

"Love doesn't understand logic.
Just feel, be kind and release over-thoughts."

"The greatest legacy we can leave behind is the feeling in your heart of gratitude, and the pure and kind love people have exchanged with you."

"Nurture is an act which will always be exchanged in unspoken or unseen ways."

"Nurturing others is the ultimate form of love and support."

"The power of nurturing others can create a ripple effect of positive change in the world."

"Nurturing others is not just a responsibility, but a gift that keeps on giving."

"The true measure of our success is in how much we have nurtured others."

"Nurturing others is not just about what we give, but how we make them feel."

The greatest impact we can have on the world is through the power of nurturing others."

"Nurturing others is the key to creating a compassionate and empathetic society."

"The more we nurture others, the more we inspire them to do the same for others."

"Nurturing others is not about fixing them but helping them to grow and flourish."

"The power of nurturing others is not just in what we do, but in the love and kindness behind it."

"The greatest gift we can give to someone is the gift of nurturing and support."

"Nurturing others is the key to creating a sense of belonging and community."

"The power of nurturing others can heal wounds that words cannot."

"Nurturing others is not just about being kind, but about showing them that they matter."

"The more we nurture others, the more we build a world filled with love and kindness."

"Nurturing others is the foundation of a healthy and positive relationship."

"The greatest strength we can obtain is in our ability to nurture and care for others."

"Nurturing others is the ultimate act of selflessness and generosity."

"The power of nurturing others can create a positive impact that lasts a lifetime."

"Nurturing others is not just about giving them what they want, but what they need."

"A great fulfillment in life of self from nurturing and supporting others."

"The pattern of care itself is another language we have to exchange with others."

"When we heal others, we fill the world with love and compassion."

"Nurturing others can heal and feed our inner child with grace."

"The power others that can transform lives was built from nurture."

"Nurturing others is the loving impact of other lives."

"The greatest joy in life comes from nurturing others through their life path."

"Nurturing others can be delivered
by guidance to pure light."

"The more we give to others, the more we build a world filled with the belief of unconditional nurture."

"Nurture is felt by being there and believing in those you are nurturing."

"One of the healing powers we have as a human is giving others our nurturing energy."

"To connect to others hearts, we nurture."

"The power of nurturing others can shift the world to a hearty legacy of love and kindness."

"We can use the power of nurture to not only change the way others feel about themselves; but to change the way we truly use our hearts."

"The way we nurture others is how
we nurture our inner child."

"Nurture can heal inner traumas which are lifetimes deep."

More from

THE ETERNAL COLLECTION

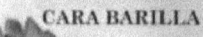

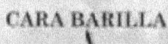

www.ingramcontent.com/pod-product-compliance
Lightning Source LLC
Chambersburg PA
CBHW011802090426
42811CB00045B/2458/J